Williamson

Woman of the Word

Audrey J. Williamson

Woman of the Word

GEORGE W. RICE

Beacon Hill Press of Kansas City
Kansas City, Missouri

10 9 8 7 6 5 4 3 2 1

Dedication

To Audrey J. Williamson, my beloved teacher and friend for more than half a century, and to her children, Joseph, Maylou, and John. All of these have been of indispensable help in the preparation of this manuscript.—George Rice

Contents

1

Train Up a Child in the Way
PROV. 22:6

Fiery revival took place in the Methodist Church in Marathon, Iowa, in 1903. Under the preaching of a holiness evangelist, Rev. Craig, Alice Johnston was converted to Christ and wholly sanctified. Her husband, Willard, was restored to full commitment to God. This transforming experience in the lives of these parents would be indelibly written in the hearts of their children.

The Johnstons' two daughters, aged four and eight, responded quickly to the new spirit in their home. Willard and Alice became godly parents. Bible reading and family worship became a vital part of their daily routine. Soon, four-year-old Audrey told her mother: "I want to happen to me what has happened to you." Alice quickly led her little girl in opening her heart to Christ. There on her knees beside the old platform rocker, Audrey became a Christian.

Alice and Willard recognized the blessings of public worship and their need for the help of the church in raising their children to love and serve God. They were fortunate in belonging to a warm, spiritual fellowship with a mature, loving pastor. Alice made sure her girls learned the meaning of the church's rituals and sacraments. More than 70 years later, Audrey would testify: "I can still feel the hand of our godly pastor, Brother Ginn, laying his hand on my head as he baptized me and prayed, 'God, use this little girl to Thy glory. Set her apart this day to Thy service.'"

Sunday School was always a happy learning and fellowship experience for Audrey. Her Sunday School superintendent asked Audrey to teach her first class when she was just 13. Audrey loved her preschool children, and she wanted to be of service to Jesus. Her desire to be useful to God helped her overcome her lack of formal training. She was able to communicate the gospel on their level, and the children quickly came to love and respect their young teacher.

During her growing-up years, Audrey's parents diligently nurtured her into a well-rounded young woman. Audrey's father had become a successful accountant in Webster City, Iowa, Audrey's hometown. He taught her his love for music, though he was not a musician or a singer himself. He exposed her to the best in all kinds of music. She remembers being sent with her sister on an 80-mile train ride to attend a special symphony. With his encouragement, she began to study violin at the age of eight and for a time looked forward to a career in music. She came to appreciate the great hymns of the church and began to memorize the lyrics. These would become a rich resource throughout her lifetime of teaching, speaking, and writing.

Audrey attributes her increasing love for prayer and Bible study to her mother's example and training. Alice Johnston was almost 40 years old when she sought and found the Savior, and she was challenged to make up for those lost years. She quickly developed an insatiable desire for God's Word. The Bible was propped above her kitchen sink as she washed the dishes, and opened on a nearby table beside her ironing board. Audrey remembers her mother down on her knees, scrubbing the large kitchen floor. Her opened Bible lay in the dry space ahead of the bucket of suds, brush, and mop. She kept reading and memorizing and pushing the Book ahead of her.

Audrey later testified that in the 30 years her mother lived after becoming a Christian, she memorized hundreds of passages and verses and became a thorough Bible student. Not content just to study the Bible for herself, Alice made Bible study and memorization a vital and regular part of her children's activities. Audrey remembers her mother's daily call from their play: "Come in, girls. It's time for Bible study."

Audrey often quotes the first verse she memorized, "I am the good shepherd: the good shepherd giveth his life for the sheep" (John 10:11). The second verse she learned was "For I will give you a mouth and wisdom, which all your adversaries shall not be able to gainsay nor resist" (Luke 21:15). Scattered verses were followed by favorite passages and chapters. Her mother's example, as much as her training and encouragement, challenged Audrey to her own lifelong quest to hide God's Word in her heart.

Alice Johnston always prayed with Audrey's father before he left for work each weekday morning. Then she would awaken her girls, and after breakfast and preparation for school, she conducted what she called the "child's altar." She taught them to read and to quote the Scriptures, and to pray aloud. She always seemed to choose the passages that would have meaning for each girl that very day. By the time Audrey was 12 years old, she had studied *Binney's Theological Compendium, A Synopsis of the Evidences, Doctrines, Morals and Institutions of Christ.* This treatise became a tremendous treasure of truth for Audrey.

Audrey later recalled that "I never backslid; my mother wouldn't let me. She taught me to correct my mistakes as soon as they happened, and helped me to pray through my problems."

Alice Johnston modeled her practical faith by a compassionate ministry to the poor of her small town. Writing a half-century later to ministers' wives, Audrey related: "I can recall as a child, that Mother was buying a coat. She was making a decision between two garments of approximately the same price. One was cut on tailored lines; the other was a bit more dressy with a little fur on the collar. We children and my father preferred the latter coat. But I can still see my mother's face, when after a moment's deliberation she said, 'I believe it will be a little easier for me to work with my poor people if I buy the plainer coat.' She did buy it, and all of us thought she was right."

Being trained as schoolteachers, both of Audrey's parents encouraged her in the love of learning and the desire for achievement. Blessed with a good mind and a growing love for academics, she graduated from high school as valedictorian of her class of about 30 students.

Audrey's young life was not all devotion and study, however. Secure in her small town, she was free to roam the surrounding fields and woods and learned to identify birds, animals, and flowers. She loved people and had many friends and playmates. Her happy childhood helped prepare her for a lifetime of useful service to God, her family, and the thousands of people who are still being touched by her life and influence.

2

Study to Shew Thyself Approved unto God
2 TIM. 2:15

Audrey's adolescent years seemed to be unmarked by the traumas young people often experience. She attributes this to her settled devotional habits, still carefully guided and encouraged by her mother. Audrey's musical talent and her gift for Scripture memory often brought her recognition in church and school. Her mother had carefully taught her to recognize that every talent she possessed was a gift from God, to be developed and used for His glory alone. Throughout her lifetime, this would help save her from the false pride and self-aggrandizement often associated with too much early public acclaim.

Audrey's parents encouraged her to enroll at the Central Holiness University in University Park, Iowa.

As a sophomore, Audrey reached another spiritual milestone. Dr. John L. Brasher, a gifted and dramatic teacher, preacher, and beloved college president, brought the chapel message one evening. Using the background of the story of the raising of Lazarus (John 11:1-45), he threw out a stirring challenge: "Who will go and call today's dead Lazari to live?"

Audrey testified that, in that moment, "A voice spoke to me." She made a full and complete consecration to God, as described in Rom. 12:1-2. She stood up, along with 40 or 50 other students, to express her willingness. Dr. Brasher next gave a "passive" appeal: "Who will go, if God calls you?" She was forever glad that she had responded to the first "active" commitment challenge, to go, "unless God stops you." For 75 years God has continued to encourage her and has never seen fit to "stop" her.

Audrey majored in speech communication with a secondary interest in music. As a senior, at age 20, she was asked to teach her major subject, and following graduation, she stayed on at the college as a communications instructor.

Audrey's father continued to be a strong guiding influence in her life. Mr. Johnston had the courage to confront his daughter when he recognized her tendency to be too opinionated. As she described one episode, following a vigorous discussion at the dinner table: "I had defended my position, I am sure, with characteristic vigor and self-assurance. Before he left for work, my father said quietly, 'Audrey, I have something to say to you. You always have to have your own way, not because it is your way, but because it is always the right way.'"

Audrey retreated to her bedroom and cried all afternoon. As she later wrote about this learning experience: "My sister and my mother came from time to time to comfort me and to tell me Papa had been too hard on me, that it wasn't really so. I was crying, not because my father had hurt my feelings. I was brokenhearted because I knew it was so. In that long afternoon, I faced up to myself and realized I was developing an intolerance, a lack of understanding love toward anyone who differed with me. All my life that experience has helped me."

Throughout her college career, Audrey was a popular student and had many "friends and escorts." During her senior year, a new student enrolled at the college, who was destined to fill a vital place in her life. Audrey had first met Gideon Williamson at a children's meeting on an

Iowa campground when she was 13 and he was 14. At the time, as Gideon described later, "We were neither one impressed by the other. I was a lanky towhead in short britches, and she a shy girl with long braids."

Gideon, feeling a call to prepare himself for some form of Christian service—perhaps as a singer—enrolled at the Central Holiness University in 1919. About this time, his older brother, Crawford, was called to be the pastor of the nearby Church of the Nazarene in Oskaloosa, Iowa. When Gideon enrolled at the college, he became a member of this Church of the Nazarene and was immediately hired as the church janitor.

Five months later Crawford Williamson died during the flu epidemic that raged across the nation. This tragic experience made a great impression on Gideon. He later testified, "I felt a deepening compulsion to live according to the will of God." He was soon led into the crisis experience of entire sanctification. In a preservice prayer meeting, as he described later, "The Spirit came in no demonstrative way, neither did I bear any public testimony to His coming, but there I told the Lord I would accept His will for me whatever it might be. There came to me there a sense of light and peace that has grown brighter and sweeter as the years have gone by."

Gideon's urgent call to become a preacher of the gospel was quickly discerned by others. His friend, D. I. Vanderpool, often described his personal joy when he recognized that "the mantle of Crawford has fallen upon Gideon." The fledgling preacher was soon called to pastor the Church of the Nazarene at Farmington, Iowa.

At the college, Gideon was often enrolled as a student in Audrey's classes. Even as a freshman, he had shown romantic interest in her, but she was slow to respond. Throughout his college years and his added pastoral years at Farmington, he occasionally dated her, but their relationship continued to be platonic.

Three things held Audrey back. Foremost, she wasn't certain it was God's will for her to give serious attention to Gideon's efforts to win her love. Even her personal feelings were subject to what she could discern was God's highest will for her life. She must have His inward assurance that any such relationship would have her Heavenly Father's approval.

Furthermore, she deeply cherished her teaching career. Marrying a preacher would mean giving up her teaching for the uncertain conditions of life in a parsonage.

Finally, she loved her Methodist Church and wasn't persuaded she should leave it. If she were to marry Gideon Williamson, she would feel honor bound to join his church and to totally support the ministry to which God had called him.

In 1927, after seven years in Farmington, Gideon was called to become the pastor of the Austin Church of the Nazarene in Chicago, Ill. Since he was single, he chose to room and board at a YMCA near the church. Though he and Audrey had had a serious disagreement before he left Iowa, he never looked in any other direction for a wife. After more than a decade, Audrey still held first place in his affections.

Audrey, meanwhile, felt the need for further education. She enrolled in 1928 at Northwestern University in the Chicago suburb of Evanston, Ill. A few months later, Gideon learned through a mutual friend that "Audrey would now welcome my attentions." Immediately, as he phrased it, "My hope and my courage both rose." They started to keep company again. When she finished her class work toward the M.A. degree, with a major in speech communication, she returned to the

Central Holiness University to continue her teaching career.

In the summer of 1929, Audrey returned to Evanston to take special classes in the newly developing field of remedial speech. These studies would be an asset to her personal ministry for many years. God would use her acquired skills to help many young people needing remedial speech therapy.

During this summer session at Northwestern University, Audrey's friendship with Gideon deepened into genuine love. One Sunday, Gideon invited Audrey to visit him and his church. It was a beautiful day of meaningful fellowship. Later that night he telephoned Audrey at her rooming house. Among other things, he said that he felt like Jacob of ancient Israel. Jacob, he told her, had worked 14 years to win his beloved Rachael, and he, Gideon, had already worked 10 years to win her affection. Then he added these plaintive words: "But Jacob had a contract, and I don't."

In that moment, a light of assurance dawned in Audrey's heart that this was indeed God's will for her life and their future. "Yes, you do," was her answer.

"Did I hear you right?" Gideon answered.

Her quiet answer was, "Yes, you did!"

"Do you really mean what you are saying?" Gideon persisted.

"With all my heart!" the young teacher responded. The happy couple decided to delay their wedding for two more years. Both had overhanging school bills, and they felt they should work and pay off these obligations before marriage. Otherwise their ministry might later be compromised. This proved to be a wise decision, for the Depression fastened its grip on the nation soon after their wedding day.

Audrey returned to Iowa that September to continue her teaching career. During this time of separation, they began what became a lifelong habit of writing a letter to each other every day they were apart. This grew into a mountain of correspondence when Gideon served 9 years as college president and 23 years as general superintendent.

Gideon Williamson and Audrey Johnston were married at the Methodist Church in Oskaloosa, Iowa, on June 6, 1931. Audrey was 31, Gideon 32. Her parents had been married on that same date in June many years before. In Gideon's words: "It was for keeps. We both had reached a point of complete dedication, not only to one another, but

22

to the full will of God as it should unfold for us."
Audrey's description was equally affirmative: "As
we drove away on our honeymoon, a deluge of
rain poured down on our secondhand Pontiac. As
I drew up closer to my bridegroom, I remember
thinking, Come rain or shine, I am doing what I
want to do. We had our measure of both rain and
shine, but I never changed my mind."

3

Thy People Shall Be My People
RUTH 1:16

After four years of effective ministry in Chicago, Gideon Williamson was called to the pastorate of the First Church of the Nazarene in Cleveland. When he accepted the call, the outstanding mortgage on the church was $55,000, plus the interest —a staggering load in that Depression day. Building operation notes had long been unpaid. There was a first and second mortgage on the parsonage as well. Gideon insisted that his $50.00 weekly salary be cut to $45.00 until other obligations were met.

He was there alone for four Sundays and then returned to Iowa for his bride. After a short honeymoon, both of the newlyweds immediately plunged into the challenging work of pastoral ministry. In Audrey's words, "I was never called to preach, but I was as called to be a pastor's wife as Gideon was to be a pastor." They lived simply on Gideon's salary. To help stretch their meager budget, Audrey cashed in the several shares of stock that her father had given her as a wedding present.

Years later, Audrey was comissioned to write a book especially for every preacher's wife. She titled this *Far Above Rubies,* from the description given in Prov. 31:10-31, a Scripture passage she had memorized while a teenager in Iowa. She pictured every pastor's wife as "a noble woman," called to an exalted task that demanded lifetime dedication. From this ancient Scripture portion, she pictured the proper response of the preacher's wife to her home, to her church, to those beyond her church, to her husband, and to herself.

The qualities she idealized had been worked out in her own life during the years when she was a pastor's wife in Cleveland, and, for a short time, in Kansas City. Whatever her husband's assignment, she lived by these principles. She was a preacher's wife of great strength, though she modestly discounted her own talents and contribution. She had great feeling for those called to the demanding life of a pastor's wife. This is the reason she wrote the following to these who gave so much:

Perhaps women of no other profession would so much desire to be known as women of strength as would the keepers of the manse. Yet what group lives a life less conducive to the development of strength, with its interruptions, its demands, its drains and strains! Women of the parsonage must purpose to be women of strength. They must will to be strong, not in one great cataclysmic experience, which would be easier, but in the day-by-day maintenance of those attitudes, the practice of those disciplines, the cultivation of those graces, and the pursuit of those ideals which will almost imperceptibly bring one to the measure of the stature of perfect womanhood.

As she did in every assignment, Audrey gave total support to her husband and pastor. She went with him on needed pastoral calls and often entertained people in the parsonage. She was especially challenged by Women's Ministries.

In their first pastorage, God placed a special responsibility on Audrey's heart. She saw a sizable group of indifferent young people who "sat on the backseat of their church, chewed gum, and whispered during every service." They were openly hostile toward being organized into any young people's society.

Audrey won them with her warmth and became their teacher. First she invited them to a campfire "corn roast," where, to their surprise, they had a wonderful time. Within a few weeks they asked their teacher if they could have another corn roast party, and perhaps be organized into a regular NYPS. She followed up by organizing a teenage orchestra to play in the Sunday services. She soon saw them move "en masse" to the front seats of the church.

Audrey wasn't satisfied until there was a spiritual breakthrough and many of those teenagers sought and found Christ. In 1990, almost 60 years after her ministry in Cleveland, Audrey still received appreciation Christmas cards from several who had been in that youth group. They have continued to serve God, and they still remember the one who helped lead them toward Christ and heaven.

During these years, Audrey rejoiced in Gideon's growing ability to preach scripturally and forcefully. His success was her success. As an elected delegate from his district to the NYPS Convention and the General Assembly of his church, he traveled to Wichita, Kans., in 1932. With just a few hours notice, he was asked to preach in the afternoon service of the NYPS Convention and on the following day was elected president of the general Nazarene Young People's Society.

In this capacity, he was called to many districts and youth conventions and received widespread recognition throughout the Church of the Nazarene. Audrey was content to stay home and care for their two children. She always looked back on these years as one of the happiest and most rewarding periods of her life. Both she and Gideon asked for nothing more than the privilege of fulfilling his pastoral call. This was not to be, however, for Gideon's abilities made him the ideal candidate for another challenge in a different but very significant area of ministry.

4

With God All Things Are Possible
MATT. 19:26

During the time the Williamsons had moved to Cleveland, events were taking place in Quincy, Mass., that would drastically affect their future. Dr. Floyd Nease was the dynamic president of Eastern Nazarene College as this fledgling liberal arts school took root and flourished. In their struggle to achieve academic accreditation, a classroom and administration building was a vital need. Under normal conditions, it would have been a relatively easy task to pay the construction cost of this project that had been completed in 1930.

Dr. Nease, however, died while on a fund-raising tour, just as the Great Depression fastened its grip on the nation. A faculty member was elected as the new president. One financial crisis followed another. Only the sacrificial service of a dedicated faculty kept the school afloat during the next few years. Most of the teachers survived only by moonlighting at various menial jobs in the community. Clouds of impending bankruptcy loomed overhead. In 1936 the president resigned due to illness.

Rev. G. B. Williamson, as he was now known, was the unanimous choice of the College Board of Trustees for their new president. Audrey and he believed they should accept this new challenge. They arrived in Massachusetts to find a decreased enrollment and low student and teacher morale. Only a fraction of the small faculty salaries was being paid, and this mostly in the form of groceries distributed from the college kitchen.

Audrey had known tough times before and adapted quickly to these circumstances. As they shared the sacrifices and individual problems of the college faculty, morale and vision for the future slowly increased.

Audrey loved teaching and had long thought this would be her lifework. She was glad that God had led Gideon and her back to the atmosphere of a Christian college. The administration immediately recruited her to teach speech communication.

Audrey was also asked to take over as the teacher of the college orchestra, a nondescript group of indifferent, undisciplined music students. They had no sense of group cooperation and little or no desire for the hard work necessary for success. Audrey accepted this challenge with the same enthusiasm she had demonstrated toward the teenage class in Cleveland. Long before her nine-year tenure was completed, they became a united group of earnest musicians who responded to skill and spirit.

Audrey remembers many nights of fervent prayer for the survival of the college. She had not realized at first that those college years would involve her husband's travel throughout the zone. He was waging an all-out campaign to eliminate an overwhelming indebtedness. She agreed completely when Gideon pledged an amount that seemed far beyond their straitened means, and she cheerfully budgeted pennies to enable the giving of those dollars.

In all of this, she was wise enough to involve her children in the thrill of sacrifice for a higher cause. This helped them to gladly share in the personal sacrifices their giving made necessary. At family devotions one morning, five-year-old Joe prayed fervently: "God bless the 'Current' fund. O God, bless the 'Special' fund." He had caught the vision.

Audrey loved to challenge the hearts and minds of eager young people, and motivate them to follow and to achieve God's best for their life. One student declared that "she could see through me like a glass window. She knew what I needed and wasn't selfish or bashful in offering her guidance." Another young man remembers his first speech in her class. When no other student would speak up to evaluate his efforts, Audrey declared: "Well, I have a suggestion. I'd like to put a stick of dynamite under you, and I'd be delighted to light the fuse." That boy never forgot her advice and later became a successful pastor and conference president in his denomination.

Audrey confesses that her greatest personal temptation was to give too high a priority to her call as a teacher. But she could never forget that her husband and her children must always have first call in her life. When the scales of her life and work seemed to be tipping too far toward teaching, God always brought her back to her first and basic calling. One of Dr. Williamson's annual duties as president was to deliver a State of the College report to each district assembly on the Eastern Educational Zone. On the day before the meeting of the New England District, he asked Audrey to go with him to Malden, Mass., saying that he needed her help with the school presentation. He requested that she recite Isaiah 40. He knew that she had memorized these 31 verses as a part of her continued Bible study program.

In those next 24 hours, Audrey reviewed and rehearsed this Old Testament passage and prayed to prepare her heart as well as her mind for this new challenge. She had often recited Scripture passages in classes and small groups, and knew she could trust her memory. She also knew how much all this could affect the attitude of pastors and delegates, whose loyalty and support was so vital to the future of the school.

Those who were present will never forget the impact of that college service. As Audrey began: "Comfort ye, comfort ye my people, saith your God," those assembled in that crowded church gave rapt attention. Their interest quickened as she reached verse 8: "The grass withereth, the flower fadeth: but the word of our God shall stand for ever." She put all of her training and skill and spirit to its highest use as she recited "Hast thou not known? Hast thou not heard, that the everlasting God, the Lord, the Creator of the ends of the earth, fainteth not, neither is weary." The audience gave a prolonged, standing ovation as she finished the last verse: "They that wait upon the Lord shall renew their strength; they shall mount up with wings as eagles; they shall run, and not be weary; and they shall walk, and not faint." The Bible had come alive through her inspired rendition. Audrey felt strongly that the applause was not for her but for God's "quick and powerful" Word, made known by the inspiration and help of the Holy Spirit.

This occasion proved to be God's opened door for Audrey to an enlarged ministry of Scripture reading all across the Church of the Nazarene. In the years ahead, as the honored wife of a college president, general superintendent, and Bible college teacher, she would be called on to verbally interpret dozens of major passages of Scripture. Not once would she allow these occasions to become mere performances, bringing recognition to her. As she studied and memorized and meditated on each Bible portion, those written words came alive to her, and she delighted to share this new meaning with others.

5

Go Ye into All the World
MARK 16:15

Dr. G. B. Williamson resigned as president of Eastern Nazarene College in May 1945. During his tenure there, the mortgage was eliminated and ENC earned accreditation, being admitted to full membership in the New England Association of Colleges and Universities. Dr. Williamson left ENC because he felt led of God to accept the call to become pastor of the First Church of the Nazarene in Kansas City.

This was a happy decision for Audrey. For nine years, Gideon's work in college administration had taken him away from home most weekends, and often for weeks at a time. Her third child had been born during their final year at ENC, and she eagerly looked forward to being able to have her husband home for supper every night. Furthermore, she knew that it was a return to his first love, the pastoral ministry.

Audrey and Gideon arrived in the Midwest at a very historic time. The Nazarene Theological

Seminary had been authorized by the General Assembly in 1944. Dr. Hugh Benner, Gideon's predecessor at First Church, had been appointed as the new president. The Williamsons came to this great church just in time to welcome the new seminary faculty and staff. Hundreds of students from around the world would soon be arriving in this headquarters city of the Nazarene denomination. The fast growing metropolis was bursting with post-WW II prosperity and opportunity. Audrey settled down happily to what they both hoped would be a longtime ministry. But it was not to be.

In March 1946, Dr. R. T. Williams died while serving as senior general superintendent. Dr. Williamson was asked to preach his funeral sermon. The *Manual* mandated that this vacancy should be filled by a mail vote of the district superintendents of the church. On the second ballot, Audrey's husband was elected. After heart-searching prayer, he responded that he would accept the election, "depending fully upon God's help."

Audrey fought one of her major spiritual battles. At this time, their children were 14, 11, and 2 years of age. Recognizing that Gideon's name was prominent in the balloting, she, characteristically, went to prayer. As she wrote later: "I did not see how I could rear the children with their father gone most of the time."

But God's grace would be sufficient. Dr. J. B. Chapman conducted an impressive induction service as this newest general superintendent began this challenging area of ministry. "Help us to follow this modern Gideon and to break our pitchers and hold up our torches," he prayed. Audrey later described: "Just then something happened to me! I felt the enabling power of God possess me! And I knew I could do whatever I had to do!"

Audrey went on to testify that, "In the 22 years my Gideon served the church as a general superintendent, I bade him good-bye hundreds of times and I spent hundreds of days away from him. But I don't believe he ever saw me shed a tear or heard me offer a word of complaint. I shed plenty of tears and I had to pray countless times for grace and wisdom. But God's visitation to me that morning was verified and renewed time after time. He did enable me to do what I had to do."

Audrey's primary task during Gideon's early years in the general superintendency was to care for their children. She faithfully kept the home fires burning, and remained active in the work of First Church in Kansas City. She taught several adult Sunday School classes and became one of the most sought-after Women's Ministry speakers in the denomination.

In 1966 Audrey was asked to serve as the early morning devotional speaker for the first International Nazarene Layman's Conference. The response was so enthusiastic that her messages based on Romans 12 were published under the title *Overcome Evil with Good.* Three times in the next 12 years she was asked to continue this ministry. "Love Is the Greatest," "Toward His Image," and "Take My Life" were her devotional themes. Each one became a best-selling book the following year.

During her years in Kansas City, Audrey agreed to teach a class to seminary students of effective Scripture reading. In class one evening she asked a student to quote the first sentence of the 23rd psalm.

The student formed the words of the familiar scripture, but no sound came from his mouth. Audrey invited the young man to stay after class and talk with her. In this interview, he told how his speech difficulty was becoming a problem. He said that he had given the Lord a few more months to cure the condition. If He didn't, then he would prepare for some other service area of ministry.

Further conferences convinced Audrey that he had a speech aphobia, a temporary loss of speech due to the failure of his vocal bands to respond in situations of stress. For several months, she worked with him until, slowly but surely, the condition was relieved.

That student would go out to lead and build what is now College Church of the Nazarene in Olathe, Kans. Paul Cunningham often acknowledges his debt to Audrey Williamson, a woman God used to confirm the direction of his life and ministry.

In May 1971, Audrey received recognition for her outstanding contribution as a woman in the church when Bethany Nazarene College conferred upon her the honorary degree "Doctor of Laws and Letters." She appreciated the recognition, but Dr. Audrey Williamson continued to be the same helpful, friendly, approachable person who had started out to give her best to God and her generation.

6

Able to Teach Others Also
2 TIM. 2:2

June 23, 1968, was a red-letter day in Audrey's life. For 24 years she had known the pangs of separation and loneliness, often when she needed her husband the most. On that final day of "G.S." responsibility, her husband laid down his administrative gavel. The appreciation of the entire church was beautifully expressed and demonstrated in their farewell service.

The Williamsons had already decided the major direction of their retirement ministry. Dr. Charles Strickland had invited them to become part of the Nazarene Bible College, recently established in Colorado Springs. Gideon and Audrey offered their teaching services without salary.

For the next 12 years, Gideon taught Bible and homiletics and Audrey taught communications and English. For several years, Gideon also was the college chaplain. Many of the students worked full-time, so the professors taught morning and evening classes. Both Gideon and Audrey often gave all or part of their treasured Saturdays as well to counsel students with special needs requiring help beyond the general classroom time.

Audrey's evaluation of this phase of their life was typical of her ideals of family and Christian service: "These years at the Bible college were probably the most rewarding of all the years of our married life. We were doing together work that thrilled us both. Every day was an adventure. We couldn't wait to report what the Lord had done in the lives of our students. We were seeing a dream fulfilled. Those were long days, for we taught both morning and evening classes. But we were given strength for our days."

Audrey was exhilarated to have her husband home for meals each day. But her most precious memories are of their Saturdays. Riding together on their Tennessee walking horses was a weekly adventure in the foothills of the Rocky Mountains. These excursions made them both realize just how much Gideon's administrative travels had cost them during their married lifetime. Now they made the most of every day and every experience. This included the preparation and editing of Gideon's classic daily devotional book *Holiness for Every Day.*

Gideon had often told Audrey that he still

wanted to take her for a tour of Latin America and the Caribbean. In 1971 they were able to make what became a challenging and relaxing three month's journey. Audrey's desire was to visit the missionaries and to see their accomplishments.

Upon their return, she assisted Gideon in writing a missionary reading book account of their trip titled *Then and Now.* She reveled in "the courage, patience, humility, submission, self-sacrifice, longsuffering, and fortitude of missionary wives." Some of these became her telephone and pen pals.

At Nazarene Bible College, Audrey continued to use her talents with the students who flocked to her classes. She was especially challenged to help those with communication disabilities, and worked hard to help them overcome physical and emotional impediments that could hinder their ministry.

Audrey rejoices in the results of her Bible college efforts. Many faithful and successful men and women of ministry owe much to her dedicated efforts. She shares in their accomplishments.

7

Her Children . . .
Her Husband . . . Praiseth Her
PROV. 31:28

Audrey Johnston and Gideon Williamson were ideally suited. Both had been reared in solid Christian homes, with parents who modeled Christ. They had both grown up around family altars, with Bible reading, study, and memorization an accepted part of their lives. Both attended a vital church, where the teaching and claims of the gospel of holiness reinforced everything they learned at home. Discipline was lovingly firm. Both had sought and found Christ as Savior at an early age. From childhood, both were challenged to make the most of their lives in whatever calling they should pursue. Both loved music enough to plan to make this their career, Audrey as a violinist and Gideon as a gospel singer. Best of all, both were totally committed to the will of God for their personal lives.

When they were married and established their home in the First Church parsonage in Cleveland, they embraced the same life-style of daily family altar that both had known since childhood. In writing to the wives of other pastors years later, Audrey described her own ideal for a truly Christian marriage: "Trust, implicit, steadfast, mutual, is the basis for the exalted relationship of marriage. Its component parts are love and confidence, born of a record of fidelity and faith. It is present at the beginning of any happy marriage. It builds up as the years prove its justification. It is a reciprocal thing, given and received by both husband and wife. It is not blind. It is a safe thing, safely placed, safely returned."

From the very first weeks of their marriage, Audrey was a working teammate in her husband's ministry. They did their best to accomplish their God-given goals and aspirations. In all of his varied later assignments, she never lost the challenge of this togetherness.

During their years in Cleveland, two children were born to Audrey and Gideon. Joseph was born on July 28, 1932. Three years later, on August 9, 1935, Maylou arrived and was named for her aunt, Audrey's sister. Both parents purposed that they would raise their family with all the wisdom and spiritual benefits they had known during their own early years. Family prayer, Bible study, and Scripture memorization became a vital part of their daily schedule.

The Scriptures played a part in the discipline of the home. When he was six years old, Joe lied to his mother. She admonished him about the evil of not telling the truth. When Gideon came home that night, he added the biblical warning that "All liars shall have their [place] in the lake which burneth with fire and brimstone" (Rev. 21:8). The child may not have understood all this strong imagery, but he certainly got the message. The next morning at family devotions, Joe ended his prayer with: "Dear Lord, help me never to tell a lie again, so I'll miss all that fire and tombstones." From that day forward, Audrey testifies, Joe might have had other problems, but he was careful to tell the truth and to be totally honest in dealing with God, himself, and other people.

Maylou learned the lessons of prayer and trust in God for all things great and small. During the rationing years of World War II, she was permitted to walk to the store to pick up a new pair of shoes that Audrey had previously ordered. Stopping to make sure she still had the money, she dropped the coupon. Checking again a while later, she discovered the loss. Panic-stricken at first, she then remembered to pray for God's help and retraced her steps. Among all the colorful autumn leaves blowing across the lawns and the sidewalk, she quickly found the missing coupon. She stopped, looked up, and thanked God for His immediate answer to her prayer. She had learned a lesson of trust and carefulness that she would never forget.

Audrey never considered herself a perfect parent. With all her background and study, she was still a lifetime learner. As she wrote in her first book, *Your Teenager and You:* This "has been both an engaging and a humbling experience. I have been reproached many times when I wrote of what I should have been rather than of what I was. I have wept, looking back at my own weakness, my failures and shortsightedness. I have asked my adolescents to forgive me, and many more times I have bowed my head over my manuscript and asked God to forgive me."

Many years later, Audrey suggested to her adult son Joseph that perhaps they had been too severe and overzealous with him in his younger days. Joe's honest answer could be echoed in the lives of most children: "Mama, if you hadn't ruled me with firm discipline, I'd have been a lost soul. I had so much of myself in me that I had to be disciplined."

Audrey's experience with her first two teenagers did not totally prepare her for rearing her youngest son, John, born in 1944, when she had just become 45 years of age. Once after reprimanding him, she encouraged him to dry his tears, and to remember that "Jesus forgives and forgets." His reply was a classic rebuke. "Then I wish you were more like Jesus. When I do something wrong, you just keep bringing it up and bringing it up." Audrey had learned another valuable lesson from her children.

Both of Audrey's sons answered God's call to be preachers of the same glorious gospel their father and mother had taught and modeled. Maylou chose to marry a preacher. At the present time, Dr. Joseph Williamson is serving as dean of the chapel at Princeton University in New Jersey. Maylou's husband, Dr. Franklin Cook, serves as regional director of missions in the Church of the Nazarene in Europe, India, and the Middle East and continues his ministry as editor of the *World Mission* magazine. The Rev. John Williamson, after serving for many years as a successful pastor and associate, is now chaplain at the Nazarene Bible College in Colorado Springs.

Over the years, Audrey has continued to nurture her children, seven grandchildren, and three great-grandchildren. Audrey identifies with a recent senior citizen who declared that: "Grandchildren are God's compensation for growing old."

At Joe's suggestion, Audrey's family happily decided on a special plan to celebrate her 91st birthday. All her children and their spouses, along with all the grandchildren and their children, gathered in Colorado Springs for a thrilling reunion. At a climactic birthday banquet, Audrey gave an unforgettable appeal to these loved ones. She reminisced about an incident from her own childhood.

In the summer when Audrey was six, her mother took her two daughters to a camp meeting held in the Boone, Iowa, city park. The campers lived in small tents, slept on army cots, and cooked over gasoline burners. Services were held in a shed called the "Pavilion," built for performances of the town band. One night Audrey awoke to see her mother fully dressed, standing at the tent flap and holding a kerosene lantern. She was watching the approach of a violent Iowa thunderstorm. Her mother's sudden command was, "Girls, get dressed and run for the Pavilion."

They quickly obeyed and joined other campers gathered there. They "entertained" themselves in singing and worship all through that stormy night. By daylight, all the tents were flat on the ground. But they had been safe in the Pavilion.

There was not a dry eye as Audrey quoted Ps. 27:5, "For in the time of trouble he shall hide me in his pavilion." She declared to her family that she "could not rest until she knew they were all safe in God's pavilion."

8

As Thy Days,
So Shall Thy Strength Be
DEUT. 33:25

Audrey and Gideon had moved to five different states during their first four decades of married life. All these changes had been made because of new challenges for her husband's ministry. Audrey had accepted every move as part of God's unfolding plan for their lives. Her journey into retirement was not made with the same joy and anticipation. For his last two years as Bible college teacher, Gideon struggled against the cancer that would eventually end his life. The lengthening shadow of his illness robbed those autumn years of much of their color and beauty.

In the summer of 1980, he and Audrey decided to move to Mesa, Ariz., to be near their son, John.

Gideon's farewell to his beloved church was as a morning devotional speaker at the General Assembly, in June 1980. Following his lifetime speaking pattern, he quoted appropriate passages of scripture from memory. His conclusion was dramatic: "I don't expect to see you at the next General Assembly. With warmest affection and sincere prayers and love for everybody, I bid you an affectionate farewell."

The retired couple returned to Colorado in October, and Gideon preached what proved to be his final sermon, at his local First Church, using Eph. 2:20-22 as his text. His family members all participated in this victorious occasion. Gideon preached with strong voice and animated delivery. But he was hospitalized a few hours later with severe internal bleeding.

During the following week, Gideon was able to attend the Bible college chapel service for the last time. The Board of Trustees had chosen this occasion to rename the Student Union Building "Williamson Center."

Audrey and Gideon desperately wanted the privilege of celebrating their Golden Wedding Anniversary together. They were privileged to do this in a private family observance in Phoenix on June 6, 1981. Again, they exchanged vows with words that had become a reality during 50 years: "For better, for worse, for richer, for poorer, in sickness and in health, to love and to cherish, till death us do part." Gideon replaced the worn, misshapen wedding band that had never been off her finger with a new golden ring inscribed, "1931 More Love 1981."

The following day, Gideon attended church for the last time. Appropriately, it was Pentecost Sunday. Their son, Joseph, preached a strong expositional sermon such as his father had modeled so many times. Many experienced a renewal of Pentecost as the Word was declared. Later, Joe wrote to his father on his birthday: "I will always be glad that I heard you preach in Colorado, and that you heard me preach in Arizona. Our shared vocation keeps me proud and humble at the same time."

Audrey needed special strength during Gideon's final months of intensifying pain and discomfort. "The words of Scripture and of the old hymns were of unspeakable comfort to me during those long days," she testified. As his conditioned worsened, she read God's Word to him by the hour. She was able to prove the truth of God's promise in 2 Cor. 12:9, "My grace is sufficient for thee." This assurance became especially real on December 30, 1981, when her husband finally made a peaceful and serene entrance into his heavenly reward.

In the months ahead, Audrey experienced the

loneliness known only to those who have had to say a final farewell to a beloved companion. Her family and friends lovingly stood by and helped to ease the hurt of separation. She found healing for grief also in writing the story of her husband's life and ministry, *Gideon, an Intimate Portrait.*

Other moves and changes eventually followed. Audrey's own health began to deteriorate. In 1989 she suffered a semiparalyzing stroke. Talking with others became a source of frustration to this specialist in communication. Caring for the basic needs of her home and getting from place to place was often a trial.

She almost lost the will to overcome this latest invasion of her happiness and well-being. For the first time in her life, she learned the meaning of severe depression. Always a woman of strength, she now had to fight constant weakness and discouragement. She had lost her treasured independence. As she described this stage, "I didn't care; I didn't even want to try." Her prayer was a resigned: "Lord, just take me home to heaven to be with Gideon."

Audrey realized her desperate need to challenge herself with a new vision. Gradually, as she regained her strength and mobility, she was again able to hope. God assured her He wasn't yet finished with her life and ministry. There was one thing she could do. She could pray! God could and would hear her as she wakened at night to pray, or as she lay on her bed to regain her strength many hours every day.

Audrey continues her lifetime habit of daily personal and family prayers, even when it is now more difficult to follow this pattern. She realizes anew that prayer was the greatest work she had ever done, the foundation of all other Kingdom efforts. "What God gives me to do, I will still be faithful to accomplish," is her continuing testimony.

Audrey tells of one recent night when she awoke and was impressed to intercede for a friend of many years. "What's his problem, Lord?" she asked. "That's none of your business," God seemed to answer. "You just pray, and leave the need and the results to Me." She prayed until God gave her inward assurance that her petition would be answered. The following week a call from that individual told of his troubled situation and of how God had completely supplied his urgent need. This pattern has become a vital part of her life.

Prayer had always been closely associated with Bible study in Audrey's mind. She searches the

Scriptures until God gives her just the right promise to claim for a specific need. Then she clings stubbornly to that Word in simple faith until she receives His answer. She still follows the pattern of reading enough to stimulate her mind, and "quicken her prayer urge." This deepened intercessory ministry has become the very language of Scripture, as she quotes God's promises in simple faith. She continues to pray imaginatively, making her communion with God not just her "shopping list" of needs, but a real dialogue with her loving Heavenly Father.

All of her life, Audrey has been able to find a challenging outlet for her spiritual drive. She lives in the faith that "My times are in thy hand" (Ps. 31:15). Refusing to live only in the past, however precious, she seeks to follow the advice of Henry Wadsworth Longfellow:

> Act, act in the living present!
> Heart within, and God o'erhead!

Audrey J. Williamson, God's "Woman of the Word" continues to live victoriously in the simple faith expressed by John Greenleaf Whitter in his poem "The Eternal Goodness":

> I know not what the future holds of marvel or surprise,
> Assured alone that life and death His mercy underlies.

Bibliography

*Williamson, Audrey J. *Far Above Rubies.* Kansas City: Beacon Hill Press of Kansas City, 1961.

*Williamson, Audrey J. *Gideon, an Intimate Portrait.* Kansas City: Beacon Hill Press of Kansas City, 1983.

*Mann, Edward S. *Linked to a Cause.* Kansas City: Pedestal Press, 1986.

Williamson, Audrey J. *Love Is the Greatest.* Kansas City: Beacon Hill Press of Kansas City, 1975.

Williamson, Audrey J. *Overcome Evil with Good.* Kansas City: Beacon Hill Press of Kansas City, 1967.

*Williamson, Audrey J. *The Living Word.* Kansas City: Beacon Hill Press of Kansas City, 1987.

Williamson, A. J. and G. B. *Then and Now.* Kansas City: Nazarene Publishing House, 1974.

*Williamson, Audrey J. *Take My Life.* Kansas City: Beacon Hill Press of Kansas City, 1982.

Williamson, Audrey J. *Toward His Image.* Kansas City: Beacon Hill Press of Kansas City, 1979.

Williamson, Gideon B. and Audrey. *Yesu Masiki Jay.* Kansas City: Beacon Hill Press, 1952.

Williamson, Audrey J. *Your Teenager and You.* Kansas City: Beacon Hill Press, 1952.

*These books are still available from Beacon Hill Press of Kansas City.